CATCHMENT

Don Barnard

heaventree

CATCHMENT

First edition 2008
© Don Barnard 2008
All rights reserved.

ISBN 978-1-906038-20-5

The cover photograph, taken by the author, shows the source of the River Avon at Naseby.

Heaventree logo design by Panna Chauhan

Published in the UK by
The Heaventree Press
Koco Building,
Spon End
Coventry
CV1 3JQ

We are grateful for the financial support of

'Avon', 'Naseby, Old Postcards', 'Evesham' (as 'Evesham Reach') and 'Ties' all appear in *10 Hallam Poets*, published by Mews Press 2005. 'Grand Union' appears in *Perhaps*, published by Cinnamon Press 2005. 'Death in Leamington (Take 2)' appeared on Boomeranguk 2003. 'Rugby' is based on a haiku that appeared in *The Independent* 2002. This collection has been completed with the support of a grant from Arts Council England (West Midlands).

For Angela.
As it always was, all of it.

CONTENTS

Naseby	9
Avon	10
Grand Union	11
Ashes to Ashes	12
Borderers	13
Rugby	14
Death in Leamington Take 2	15
The Kingmaker's Rule Applies	16
The Saxon Mill Restaurant, Warwick	17
Joseph Arch	18
Think On My Words	19
Lapwing	20
Abbot Lichfield's Gate	21
Old Postcards, Evesham	22
Norn	23
Home	24
Blossom Junkies	25
Watersheds	26
And So It Goes	27
Cotswold	28
Hampton Ferryman	29
Jubilee Bridge, Fladbury	31
On Bredon	32
Non Ophelia, Sed Brenda	33
Water Rights	34
Eckington Bridge	35
Strensham	36

Flood Plain	37
Windfalls	38
Space in the Bed	39
Tewkesbury Abbey	40
Water Clock	41
Ties	42
Notes to the Poems	43

Naseby
(source of the Avon)

a beginning
but quickened already,
not needing this cast-iron
omphalos
weighting its navel for meaning,
not needing naming, a snake by Lalique
sleeking the grass down a hillside
and creasing the meadows, shape-
shifting always, gleaning from ditches
the staling of cattle,
battle-spill,
dewfall and rain,
mocking the strait-laced Grand Union, wrong-
footing Rugby,
wrapping in cadences Stratford and Eckington,
drifting through shires greening in backwaters,
ending arriving at Severn
not really an ending, no more a beginning,
all water, all flowing
and all of us liquid, the heel-taps of history,
carrying in us a salting of Naseby's
lacrimae rerum,
the spittle and weeping of princes
retreating, the seep of a wen,
the last spilling of men
returning to their undoing again
and again and never
an ending

Avon

What would you call it, this slip-skinned muscle
straining at lock and lashers, stretching between?
The rooted men, who needed nothing more,
have called it *"River"*. Those who always thought
of elsewhere might have chosen *"Swan-road"*.
You might call it *"Eel"*, for its dark length,
the strength it hides till caught under mill-wheels
it thrashes to be free. *"Eel"* would be good.

Those are the easy words, the point-and-tell.
The river's juice escapes between their fingers.
It doesn't change; it changes all the time
in ways well-known to men who wake to it
or watch at nights, negotiates its banks
season by season, giving only to take.
Maybe they would call it *"Slake"* or *"Sudden"*.

It persists. It has a quality of bees
summering, wet-lipped cattle lifting their heads,
birds skimming like pebbles into reeds
or calling boundaries. So, *"Soul"* maybe.

Or a name that bears the burr of English deepening
to the west, catching the heron's beat and glide
and all the river's burdens. Such a word.

Grand Union

He was like one of those old barges
working the slow peristalsis of locks,
just passing through.
He would lie up for the night reluctantly,
tying up to terra firma
but slipping his moorings early.
He lived only in movement,
no fixed abode and carrying all his tidy needs,
at home everywhere.

He didn't travel as the crow flies,
but clung to vantage like a circling albatross,
approaching unexpectedly
and from the wrong direction.
A port and lemon in every girl
until he found a berth.

He traded them fabulous things,
monsters and miracles, godlings from Timbuktu,
paying his way with tales from his painted argosy,
the regular throb of his voice filling them, stilling
only when he legged it down the long tunnel of night.

His was a parallel universe
you only glimpsed from bridges or the train.
Truanting urchins and men in caps
walking the short way to the match
knew him to wave to, shuttling his other, narrow world
with a whiff of smoke,
a wake of used condoms and rainbows.

Ashes to Ashes

Scattering, an act of adulthood.

Dad, with his Cotswold *bist*s and *byunt*s,
and Mum, who blazed at the very name of Rome,
broadcast, like Wycliffe's ashes
carried swiftly into Avon,
drunk by all who took their water
from that English river.

All that they said and were, sunk in,
absorbed,
like the blood and bone
Dad spread on the land each Spring.

No-one now to intercede,
just me and consequences.

Borderers

Armies hesitate at rivers.
Costume and custom change.
Coinage. Little else.

These boundaries are laced with fords.
A voice low across water
and we wade in at dusk
for strange meadows.
Bank to bank,
astride
and side-saddle,
we ride in both directions,
reiving our business.

Sometimes, eventually,
we build a bridge.
Trade. Settle.

Rugby

Rules? It all began
by breaking rules, so they're few
and heeded little,

like Tartar polo
fought on foot with a dead pig,
less sport than battle,

on a muddy field
sown with lions' teeth, watered
with blood and spittle,

large, ungentle hands
carrying our breath away
in a skin bottle.

Death in Leamington (Take 2)

The Body Shop, the Woolwich, Dixons, Marks—
we have nothing to lose but our chains. The retail horde
have named and shamed the old, stuccoed façades
(still peeling and dropping, but that's stucco, John.

Built on the cheap, gone downhill ever since).
There's an Art Deco front to Pizza Hut,
a mock-Elizabethan yuppy pub,
a bank (a bank !) where Mytton, twelve years drunk,
spurred his horse upstairs, hurdled the port
and then decanted, balcony to street.
Cundall's Town Hall is even less discreet—
Tudor/Baroque, complete with campanile—
seriously funny. Victoria's not amused,
of course, but Jerry's bomb moved her an inch.
—*Oh Albert ! Albert !* —How the stucco flew !

They've closed the Pump Room baths, the fine Hammam.
Old Robbin's Baths, the Parthenon, both dry.
Lord Aylesford's Well is gone. It's a spa town;
upped then dried. They paint the stucco white.

The Kingmaker's Rule Applies

Now and then,
when he talks to God and thinks God answers
or lends his ear to charlatans and chancers,
when he's sent braver men to die
for the wrong cause with a base lie,
when he has tongued a great fool's hole because he's strong
and buried little men in dung,
or limed the perch with promises and lies
then, when he's caught his bird,
thought overmuch of plucking and of pies,
too little of his word,
when honesty's his tool of last resort,
in short
when he's a far too petty king
and you grow weary of his shit-eating grin,
you have to start again.

The Saxon Mill Restaurant, Warwick

Where waggoners, once, weighted the sack-hoist
and millers hoppered harvests and fed them
to runner and bedstone and bled them to flour,

where the paddles under pounded up-river
with pit-wheel and wallower creaking and winding
the great spur-wheel's grumbling thunder,
the whole show plain-speaking in oaken,

there's this tricksy madam, tarted with logos,
plying her trade
grinding away at Avon's old corn.

Joseph Arch
(founder and president
of the Agricultural Labourers' Union 1872)

The meadows here were hay-wained then
but Barford was no oil painting.
Some threadbare grazing, gravelly plough
in corduroy and hobnail boots
and in back-lanes, labourers cowed
to treadmill days by a thousand years
of bit and spur, parson and squire,
the Parish a cough and a sneeze away.
Joe's flint would set those fields on fire,
tinder in every ditch and hedge.

His one-eyed cottage still out-stares
the rectory across the street.
Still there, the neatly mannered plots
that put on airs on Barford Hill,
the frank two-up-two-downs that straggle
to the bridge or Wellesbourne way.
Built of metaphors, this place.
Settled in the Joseph Arch
to cottage pie and HP sauce,
you look for poems in your beer.

That square frame and head remind you—
trousers raffia'd at the knee,
waistcoat and shirt; his arms yea-thick
from tilting with the one-wheel hoe
down rows of sprouts while you wrestled
the Ferguson; how he picked vics,
always a tree ahead to show you,

knowing you wouldn't keep the ground
and gutted at the thought. Like Joe,
his Union scattered and let down
by his own. Guilt and HP sauce.
Now pick the poem out of that.

Think On My Words
(Cymbeline Act 1, Scene 5)

His nutmegged syllables,
sharp and sweet,
can startle still,
like a slow lick in a dark cellar
where the ooze and jazz of it all
glisten from the walls.

After mothers' milk,
his well-mulled English ale
comes hot and spiced.
In the spillings of words
on boards of English oak,
he traced men
as a child copied letters
in a criss-cross horn-book.

With him, the liquor of English thickened,
setting into new crystals.

Lapwing

Peewit, Dad called it, or *Old maid*. No reason why,
except that his dad did, and his. They used the easy
place-bound words, the shibboleths, names that are sly

soundings for tongues that don't belong here. All Dad's peas
were *pays*, his beans were *byuns*, he always said *I cossunt*
not *I can't*. His words were oral histories,

like when *I'm not* became the much more blunt *I byunt*,
echoes of older tongues, like *lapwing, lappewincke*,
Anglo Saxon's *læpi wince*, words that meant

it raised and dropped its crest, nothing to do with wings.
The name we give this bird—*lipwingle, lymptwigg, peesie,
wallock* or *wallop, chewit, pywipe, horneywinks*—

places each of us, tells where we first saw the easy
blink of their deceit tumbling white and black
above our childhood's fields like blossom blown from peas,

like salt and pepper for our tongues, holding that smack
of home, one of the fifty tell-tale names for *flapjack*.

Abbot Lichfield's Gate

There were other gates that had their purposes;
a Great Gate on the green where the road turned
downhill to Hampton ferry, for visitors
too grand to dismount till they'd looked down
on the abbot; a humbler gate towards the market,
for townsfolk; a snicket gate concealed
behind the kitchen midden, where the Black Monks
and abbey servants passed each day to garden
or fish Fridays in pools above the river.
Practical gates that changed no-one at all.

The abbey's gone, but Lichfield's blunt reminder
still points to the sky, challenging you
to thread its shadowed eye and be unchanged.
A gate to nowhere but heaven, to the graveyard,
it narrows down your view, intensifies beyond.
You emerge, as the monks did, blinking in doomsday.

Old Postcards, Evesham

Underneath the trees in Abbey Park,
perambulating mothers, booted, boatered, rowing-boated men,
hooped and sailor-suited children, Shippams sandwiches all gone

to condescending swans, Brummies cake-walking aboard
the *Lilybyrd*, *King George* and *Saucy Sue* at two bob down to Fladbury—
one hoot and off

around the keep-you-guessing bends, over the chain
at Hampton Ferry, past Boat Lane and the cricket ground,
past Clark's Hill and Chadbury Mill, ahead of them

the *Bee*, the *Wasp*,
stern-low with corn from here to Tewkesbury, ahead of them,

the hauliers,
half a dozen to the tow, ahead of them

more ghosts,
too faint—

birds of summer singing their long, long way downstream
to where the boatman turns against the river's will and theirs.

Norn

```
                          A
                         cool
                         sun,
     mist              on the                river,
                       coots
                       calling
                       danger
     and             out of the              mist,
                       Urth
                       comes
                       dipping,
   pulling,            dipping,             working
                       herself
                       into my
                       tapestry
    stitch              upon                 stitch


     and                                      then


      is                                      gone
                          .
```

Home

It must have hills tilting at one end of the street
that tell the weather at a glance, and a slow river
at the other you can wade, most of the year.
The High Street must be wide enough for cattle.

The station should be used occasionally, for outings,
and by locals coming in from halts to market.
There should be real bookshops, with one copy of everything
and three or more of none. And other shops, I suppose.

It must have alleyways tacking between the streets,
where people used to walk before the streets were there,
and still walk, because it's the shortest way
or because they always have.
It should have small, old churches, to match their congregations,

The young will have faith in distant things, in places
seen Saturdays before the main attraction, places
where they're allowed to do they're not sure what,
but everything they can't do now, or think they can't.

The school must turn out farmers, market gardeners, tradesmen,
inspiring some to leave all that behind because they can.
The sort of place you leave that isn't there when you go back,
the one you spend your whole life looking for.

Blossom Junkies

The orchards score the Vale
in lines like snow, like poppies
scarred for milk. Till the pale
blossom blows and drops
its angel dust, we sniff,
are hooked, each high not quite
enough, not quite enough,
but out of our heads on white.

Watersheds

They are not to be measured
in fathoms of oolite looted by raindrops,
the slumping of lias to slopes of repose, the shift
of meanders down-river,

but in faces forgotten and pledges still owing,
betrayals and night sweats, bad choices,
the jostling of birthdays.

They're measured in cycles repeated till broken,
in harvest and fallow, nettles and crop marks,
fill-dyke and parchment,
the shackles of birthrights,
"and Son" on the van,

where anything else means crossing the ridgeline
while heads shake and beds murmur
late in the night and you're still on a down-slope
with rivers that don't taste of home.

They're measured in how far you've come from your earthing,
in how much it hurts you to know.

And So It Goes

Level the weir. Open the sluice.
Leave the lock gate out of use
and let the river's hair flow loose,
for April's all about
and all about is full of juice
and juice will out.

Sing-ding, sing-dong, let bells be rung
all evening long. The year has swung
to Spring and courtship games, when young
men leap through Beltane's fire
and cinnamon fingers, garlic tongue
first learn the lyre.

Cotswold

There's one English river running north
from its source to its mouth, a dozen miles due north.
Just one. Take the long way round to find it.
From Mickleton, make your way south with the scarp on your left.
Stick to the spring line of villages spilling like scree
off the wold, a picket of places that stake out the Vale:

Aston and Weston Subedge (the locals weight it
'cabbage', not 'Savoy'), Saintbury, high as may be,
then the great green at Willersey, ruined Broadway,
Buckland and brook after brook down to Winchcombe, nudged
to the west by the strike of the hills. Soft-focus churches
and cottages rain-licked and lichened to butter and honey,

but the council houses are hard-edged, and sprouts
like nubs of splintered rock rub fingers raw
in the black frost on the tops, and snapping foxes
rip the lambs before they know their legs,
and the thick wet soil clags boots,
the chill of winter ditching kills the feet.

Salt and sweet, the hills. You can have enough.
At Waterhatch, where the beech hangers reach
for the rooks ragging loud on the updrafts,
leave the sheep-ticked ridge and furrow, seeking
Avon, bearing on Isbourne needling north
and picking up the brooks that you have crossed.

Hampton Ferryman

I'll be redundant soon.
July in Maspalomas, I met my old pal Dune,
an easy coming,
easy going kind of guy.
Too laid back for some
but can he shoot the breeze! Oh my!

"Led Alexander's rag-time band
from Oxus to Euphrates.
Great team,
me and old Sandy!"
"Hung out in the Empty Quarter. Got real high."
"Met Muhammad, more than halfway."
"Moseyed on across Sinai."
Crap like that, all day.

Hadn't seen him since I surfed the Great Sand Sea
and then in he blows to Playa del Ingles,
and we get blasted, him and me—
Moroccan red, the local black. He says
he's waiting till the wells run dry.
When the bougainvillea and hibiscus die,
he'll suck their bones and blow
hot sand in villas' empty eyes,
tap out his rhythms on men's skulls.

"Then they'll let my people go,"
he tells me. *"Liberation-wise,*
attrition's cool.
All parties end, the moment passes.
When I've burst Man's last balloon
he'll call me Mister Dune
and sue for peace
and I'll say, 'Man ! Release
the brothers from their hour-glasses.
Your eggs are over-done.
Let the sands run!'"

Tells me he's coming here one day.
Time to think of Number One.
With Dune around, it's safe to say
my ferrying days are done.
Avon will be a wadi
where the living drink their piss
and you lot cross dry-shod.
Mind how you step ashore. Thanks for the obolus.

Jubilee Bridge, Fladbury

No lamb was killed. No rams-horn trumpets blew.
Instead, they threw an iron-latticed bridge
across the river here. Top hats, po-faces,
speeches, 'God Save the Queen' off-key, applause.

Clapped out in less than fifty years, replaced
by this hop, skip and a jump in rusting steel
they still call "Jubilee", the name outlasting
cheap Victorian iron, the way words will.

There are no bridges in the Good Book. If only
they'd put their faith in sin and spilled offerings,
spoiled virgins, got fighting drunk. Then,
when they'd slept it off, buried gold and cockerels
in the footings, bribing the old gods
to smile on what they built. As they did, anyway.

On Bredon

'Twas summertime on Bredon
and love had filled our sail
with wind-borne changes
that swept us on, a gale
of song nor'westering the Vale.

We rode it out together.
It spent while you and I
were coming, coming, coming
beneath a lark-flung sky
and youth went sailing by.

Non Ophelia, Sed Brenda

You were thigh-deep, you said, and pissed,
and the cold river flooding,
thigh-deep, a red sun in the mist
and a bad marriage ending.

Two lads, you said, and you couldn't die
with someone there watching.
Angels, you said. Anglers, may be,
but your faith in them catching.

Water Rights
(for Sir William Russell, Bart.)

What millers only borrow
and the pike knows with its flank,
as soon own dawn or sparrow
as this headstrong furrow.

Cut withies from the willow,
and call them yours, perhaps,
but not pool and shallow.
Owning will follow,

the widest stream too narrow
once water is outgrown,
so drink now, drown your sorrow.
Kill for it tomorrow.

Eckington Bridge

To build a bridge, you first construct a form
to bear its weight until the keystones lock,
erect and brace a framework, something firm
to stand on, rig a hoist with rope and block,
all this before you start. You quarry stone,
then square it off and facet it to fit,
mix mortar, lay abutments, one
on either side, and wait until they've set.
Then you can build away for all you're worth,
springing the arch until it meets above,
complete, till it stands more solid than earth
and carries you, however burdened, over.

Those cautious years, was that what we were at?
A form of friendship framed in rhyme and a strong
slow bonding of trust each side. Was that
for this exquisite arching, all along?

Strensham

Sir HUDIBRAS is still devout
though Strensham church has locked him out.
Hungry souls no longer throng
to morning prayer nor evensong.
No solemn mass from priest or pastor,
the fashion now is wholly faster.
Strensham's services still thrive,
across the field on the M5
and here Sir H partakes ungrudgin'
with followers of the New Religion.

Flood Plain

                Rising,
              up before
           daybreak, dark
         sunshine lacquering
       asphalt, finding the edges
     of pavements by touch, Avon
    fingers through air-bricks and feels
   across thresholds, nudges the keels of
  bungalows beached on the flood plain, beats
 its bounds at the old benchmarks on ridges, rising.
Morning surprises them banging on ceilings or gurning
at windows, years, years in the drowning, clutching at flotsam,
 gazebos and decking and patio tables gone turning downstream,
like
       so
                many
                              cocktail
                                              sticks

Windfalls

An orchard grows where Yorkist axes pruned
Lancaster's rose and scattered, red on red
in Bloody Meadow's bowl, a *pot pourri*
of open-petalled heads.

But now we garden anywhere but here.
Whole deserts bloom. No rose as garlanded
with red, no *pot pourri* could cloy as soon
as petals that we shed.

Beneath the trees the dead, all cider-sour.
Each apple is a baby's severed head
with wasps like shrapnel burning in the eyes.
Be careful how you tread.

Space in the bed

Like a garden after snow,
no trace now of the dancing, the bonfire we built,
only this wintry acreage where nothing grows,
chilling even summer nights
when it and I lie empty
and unlovered.

Tewkesbury Abbey

As the monk, Echo,
sounding his responses in the choir,
requires no answer,
always follows on,
there are two worlds, psalm and antiphon,
and you are bound to one.

As the two ends of a bridge. Cross it
and the river flips polarity.
Specks of iron in your brain, fixed now,
make one bank feel like home, the other
not, and yet, you cross.
There must be extraordinary things.

You've crossed and seen them all.
This far downstream, the bridges cease.
There will be no more wonders.
It's years now since you learned that it must end.
Your doppelgänger told you, looking like your Dad at first,
dead and the plums half-picked,
later like your Mum, mid-breath in alabaster.

Nowadays, he plays the Scouser, dry
as bones, McGough on downers, Larkin
doing Ringo Starr. He hums Gerry
and the Pacemakers, "*Ferry,
'cross the Mersey,*" loitering
in the chancel, while you chant
antiphons, wanting more than silence,
after.

Echoes, at least.

Water Clock

The clepsydra drips.
I am timed and unmanned
by this small-hours dribbling.

In March, I peed
six feet up the lavvy wall,
in June pissed hard and long
on greening porcelain back of pubs,
in August was excused en-suite
and smelt asparagus.
October, once, I sent a goatish arc
from crags on Algarin, wetting the wind
on a vulture's wings.

November now, I'm filling furtive jugs in cubicles,
sweet waters passing, passing.
All my bluffing and bravado
narrow down to this single whether,
a winterbourne that one day will run dry.

Ties

Think of it as a rope
untied, a halyard
sliding through the ruined eyes of mills.
Gripped tightly nowhere, it slips
through wick and ford and by,
through ham and bury
falling to the sea.

Or a silk cord,
beaded with place-names.
As I tell its rosary now,
river-born and rarely
a Pater Noster from its banks,
something inside me grips
and will not let it slip as easily.
Like de Montfort,
who had England by the throat and almost won,
or the mud of Dead Man's Ait,
where Leicester's Welsh were heaped ten deep, they say.
Grips more tightly every year,
like a gland round an old man's stream,
an Avon man
claiming what he cannot own or bind,
what owns and binds him.

Or a string,
stretched and stopped
at just that point where,
plucked,
it resonates in heart and bone and gut.
No other river's like enough
to play you in that way,
yet all are like to waken longings,
thin harmonics of belonging
somewhere.